The New Mental Health Act

A guide to the appeals process

© Crown copyright 2006

ISBN: 0-7559-5127-0

Scottish Executive
St Andrew's House
Edinburgh
EH1 3DG

Produced for the Scottish Executive by Astron B48263 09/06

Published by the Scottish Executive, September, 2006

Further copies are available from
Blackwell's Bookshop
53 South Bridge
Edinburgh
EH1 1YS

The text pages of this document are printed on recycled paper and are 100% recyclable

THE NEW MENTAL HEALTH ACT
A guide to the appeals process

In March 2003 the Scottish Parliament passed a new law, the Mental Health (Care and Treatment) (Scotland) Act 2003. It came into effect in **October 2005**. It sets out how you can be treated if you have a mental disorder and says what your rights are.

This guide is one of a series about the new Act. It explains when you can appeal to the Tribunal, the Sheriff Court or the Court of Session.

The Act says
- When you can be given treatment against your will
- When you can be taken into hospital against your will
- What your rights are
- What safeguards are there to make sure your rights are protected

This guide is written for people who have a mental disorder, but it may be of interest to others including carers and independent advocates.

Disclaimer

While we have done our best to see that the information contained in this guide was accurate and up to date when it was published we cannot guarantee this. If you have any questions about how the information might apply to you, you should discuss your concerns with a solicitor, your independent advocate or other appropriate adviser.

Contents

1 Some terms used in this guide
2 Guiding principles
3 What is an appeal?
4 When can I appeal to the Tribunal?
- Short-term detention
- Compulsory treatment order (CTO)
- Orders related to criminal proceedings/offence
- Security levels
- Transfer to a hospital in Scotland
- Transfer to a hospital outside Scotland
- Appeal against unlawful detention

5 When can I not appeal to the Tribunal?
6 When can I appeal to the Sheriff Court or Court of Session?
7 Role of the Mental Welfare Commission
8 Further information contacts
9 Acknowledgements
10 Other guides in this series

1 Some terms used in this guide

The Act: The Mental Health (Care and Treatment) (Scotland) Act 2003.

The Adults with Incapacity Act (AWI): The Adults with Incapacity (Scotland) Act 2000.

Compulsory Treatment Order (CTO): this is an order which is granted by the Tribunal. It can include a number of different requirements including detention in hospital, compulsory treatment and attending services in the community. It will last initially for 6 months and can be renewed for a further 6 months, then for periods of 12 months.

Compulsion Order (CO): an order made by the court which authorises compulsory measures (either hospital or community based) for a period of 6 months, if not otherwise renewed.

Emergency Detention Certificate: this type of power authorises detention in hospital for no more than 3 days.

Hospital Direction: an order made by the court in addition to sentence of imprisonment. It allows the person to be detained in hospital for treatment of their mental disorder and then transferred to prison to complete their sentence once hospital treatment in no longer required.

Independent Advocate: under the Act anyone with a mental disorder has the right to access an independent advocate. An independent advocate is able to give support and help to enable a person to express their own views about their care and treatment.

Interim Compulsion Order: an order made by the court which authorises hospital detention for 12 weeks (but can be renewed regularly for up to one year) so that the court can gather further specific evidence on the person's mental condition.

Interim Compulsory Treatment Order: an order granted by the Tribunal which authorises compulsory measures for a period of up to 28 days. The Tribunal can make more than one interim CTO as long as the total time is not more than 56 days.

Mental disorder: this is a term used in the Act which covers mental illness (including dementia), a learning disability or a personality disorder.

Mental Health Officer (MHO): this is a specially trained social worker who deals with people with mental disorder and has particular duties under the Act.

Mental Health Tribunal: the Mental Health Tribunal for Scotland was set up by the Act to make decisions about the compulsory care and treatment of people with mental disorder.

Named Person: this is someone who will look after the person's interests if he or she has to be treated under the Act.

Responsible Medical Officer (RMO): this is the medical practitioner, usually a consultant psychiatrist, who is responsible for a person's care and treatment.

Short-term Detention Certificate: this power authorises detention in hospital and compulsory treatment for up to 28 days.

Transfer for Treatment Direction: as order made by the Scottish Ministers to allow transfer of a prisoner to hospital for treatment of a mental disorder.

2 Guiding principles

The main aim of the principles is to ensure that you are treated with respect.

Anyone who is carrying out duties, or giving you treatment, under the Act, e.g. doctors, nurses and social workers, has to follow the principles set out in the Act. They must take account of:

- your past and present wishes about your care and treatment, giving you information and helping you as much as possible to participate in decisions about this
- the views of your named person, carers, guardian or welfare attorney, if you have them
- the range of options available for your care and treatment
- what will ensure the maximum benefit for you
- making sure that you are not treated any less favourably because you are being treated under the Act
- your individual abilities and background, and other factors such as your age, gender, sexual orientation, religion, racial origin or membership of any ethnic group.

Any restrictions on your freedom should be the minimum necessary in the circumstances.

Where it is reasonable and practical, your carers' needs should be taken into account and your carers should receive information that might help them to care for you.

The services that you receive should be appropriate for your needs. Where you stop being treated under the Act, you should continue to receive care and treatment for as long as is necessary.

Where you are a child, or young person under the age of 18, people carrying out duties under the Act must try to ensure that they do what is best for your welfare.

3 What is an appeal?

If you are made subject to compulsory measures under the Act you have rights to ask the Tribunal to end or change the compulsory measures. In most circumstances your named person also has rights to appeal to the Tribunal on your behalf.

You should think about whether you would like a lawyer to assist you with this appeal. Your MHO can help provide you with a list of lawyers to help you contact a lawyer if you do not already have one.

You or your named person or your lawyer should tell the Tribunal that you want to appeal against your order. This appeal must be made in writing to the Tribunal who will need some details about you. Your appeal should include:

- your name and address
- your named person's name and address
- if you are in hospital the name and address of the hospital
- if you have to stay at a specified place, detailed in your order, the address of that specified place
- a brief summary for the reason for your appeal.

The Tribunal will arrange a hearing which you and your named person will be invited to attend. Your RMO and MHO and anyone else with an interest in your case will also be invited to attend.

4 When can I appeal to the Tribunal?

Short-term detention

You and your named person can apply to the Tribunal to have this detention cancelled.

Compulsory treatment order (CTO)

If you are on a CTO you and your named person can ask the Tribunal to change or cancel your order. (If your appeal is unsuccessful you can make further appeals although the act sets a limit on the number of appeals you can make in any year.) In general you cannot appeal until you have been on the order for 3 months.

Orders related to criminal proceedings/offence

If you are on a compulsion order you and your named person can appeal to the Tribunal to:

- be conditionally discharged
- cancel the restriction order
- cancel the restriction order and change the measures set out in your compulsion order
- cancel the compulsion order.

If you are on a compulsion order with restrictions you and your named person can appeal to the Tribunal to cancel the order or to vary the conditions of the order.

If you are on a transfer for treatment direction or a hospital direction you can appeal to the Tribunal against your detention in hospital. If you are successful you will return to prison to serve the remaining part of your prison sentence. There are time limits on when you can first appeal and how often you can appeal in any year.

Security levels

From 1 May 2006 if you are in the State Hospital and subject to a CTO, compulsion order (with or without restrictions), a hospital direction or a transfer for treatment direction you will be able to appeal to the Tribunal that you are being held in conditions of greater security than are necessary for your care and treatment. Other people can also appeal on your behalf. These are:

- your named person
- any guardian or welfare attorney you may have
- the Mental Welfare Commission.

If you are successful the hospital will have to transfer you to a hospital with more suitable security for you. A place must be found for you within the time set by the Tribunal. If not, the hospital will need to tell the Tribunal and a further hearing will be held.

If you are a restricted patient Scottish Ministers will have to agree the hospital you are to be transferred to is suitable.

Transfer to a hospital in Scotland

If your RMO thinks that you should be transferred to another hospital in Scotland for care and treatment for your mental disorder and you do not wish to go, then you or your named person can appeal to the Tribunal against this transfer. If you are successful and the transfer has taken place the Tribunal can order that you are transferred back to the hospital you were in before the transfer.

If you are transferred to the State Hospital you must make your appeal within 12 weeks of being told or of the transfer taking place (if you were not told about the transfer in advance). If the transfer is to a hospital other than the State Hospital you must make your appeal within 28 days.

Transfer to a hospital outside Scotland

If your doctor tells you that he/she is considering transferring you to a hospital in another country, and you do not wish to be transferred, you should inform Scottish Ministers of your wishes or preference about the proposed move. This must be done within 7 days of being formally told about your transfer. You can appeal to the Tribunal against the proposed move. You cannot be transferred until the Tribunal has decided your appeal. (You cannot appeal to the Mental Health Tribunal for Scotland after you have been transferred. However, you will have rights to appeal to the Tribunal or court in the country to which you have been transferred.)

Appeal against unlawful detention

If you are in hospital, but not subject to a compulsion under the Act, you should be able to discharge yourself from the hospital when you wish. If for any reason this appears not to be the case you and a number of other people on your behalf can apply to the Tribunal for an order requiring the hospital managers to discharge you.

These people are:

- your named person
- if you are a child, any person who has parental responsibilities for you
- a mental health officer
- the Mental Welfare Commission
- any guardian or welfare attorney who has been appointed under the Adults with Incapacity Act to look after your interests
- any other person having an interest in your welfare.

5 When can I not appeal to the Tribunal?

You cannot appeal to the Tribunal if you are placed on an emergency detention order.

You cannot appeal to the Tribunal if you are on an interim CTO or interim CO. However, the Tribunal has to hold a hearing to consider the interim order within 28 days of making the order. You will be able to make your views known at that hearing.

If you are on remand and transferred to hospital for assessment or treatment (or convicted but awaiting final disposal of your case) you cannot appeal to the Tribunal as the court is still considering your case.

6 When can I appeal to the Sheriff Court or Court of Session?

When the Tribunal provides you with information about its decision after a hearing it will also tell you how and to whom you can appeal that decision if you are unhappy with it. This applies to decisions on compulsion and to decisions on appeals.

This appeal right will be to the sheriff principal or in some circumstances to the Court of Session. You must make the appeal within 21 days of the tribunal's decision.

If an appeal is successful, the court will either substitute its own decision for that of the Tribunal (where it is possible to do so) or send the case back to the Tribunal to consider afresh.

If the sheriff makes an order for your removal to a place of safety you or another person with an interest in your welfare can appeal to the sheriff to end or to vary the order. This must be done within 72 hours of the order being made.

7 Role of the Mental Welfare Commission

You can contact the Commission if you want information and advice about your care and treatment rights. If the Commission has concerns about your treatment and care, it will look into your case. The Act says that the Commission still has the power to review and revoke your order. It will only use this power in exceptional cases. In general the Commission will refer your case to the Tribunal and will inform the Tribunal of any concerns it may have about your treatment and care.

8 Further information contacts

Bipolar Fellowship Scotland
Studio 1016, Abbeymill Business Centre, Seedhill Road, PAISLEY PA1 1TJ
telephone: 0141 560 2050
website: www.bipolarscotland.org.uk

Depression Alliance Scotland
3 Grosvenor Gardens, EDINBURGH EH12 5JU
telephone: 0131 467 7701
website: www.depressionalliance.org

Mental Health Tribunal for Scotland
1st Floor, Bothwell House, Hamilton Business Park, Caird Park,
HAMILTON ML3 0QA
telephone: 01698 390 000
service user and carer freephone: **0800 345 70 60**
website: www.mhtscot.org

Mental Welfare Commission for Scotland
Floor K, Argyle House, 3 Lady Lawson Street, EDINBURGH EH3 9SH
telephone: 0131 222 6111
service user and carer freephone: **0800 389 6809**
website: www.mwcscot.org.uk

National Schizophrenia Fellowship (Scotland)
Claremont House, 130 East Claremont Street, EDINBURGH EH7 4LB
telephone: 0131 557 8969
website: www.nsfscot.org.uk

The Office of the Public Guardian
Hadrian House, Callendar Business Park, Callendar Road, FALKIRK FK11XR
telephone: 01324 678 300
website: www.publicguardian-scotland.gov.uk

People First (Scotland)
77-79 Easter Road, EDINBURGH EH7 5PW
telephone: 0131 478 7707
website: www.peoplefirstscotland.com

Scottish Association for Mental Health (SAMH)
Cumbrae House, 15 Carlton Court, GLASGOW G5 9JP
telephone: 0141 568 7000
website: www.samh.org.uk

Scottish Commission for the Regulation of Care
11 Riverside Drive, DUNDEE DD1 4NY
telephone: 0845 60 30 890
website: www.carecommission.com

Scottish Consortium for Learning Disability (SCLD)
The Adelphi Centre, Room 16, 12 Commercial Road, GLASGOW G5 0PQ
telephone: 0141 418 5420
website: www.scld.org.uk

Scottish Independent Advocacy Alliance
138 Slateford Road, EDINBURGH EH14 1LR
telephone: 0131 455 8183
website: www.siaa.org.uk

Scottish Public Service Ombudsman
4 Melville Street, EDINBURGH EH3 7NS
Telephone: 0870 011 5378
Website: www.scottishombudsman.org.uk

Your local authority is listed in the telephone directory under council services.

9 Acknowledgements

This guide was produced in collaboration with Scottish Association for Mental Health, National Schizophrenia Fellowship Scotland, the Scottish Independent Advocacy Alliance, the Mental Welfare Commission for Scotland, the State Hospital at Carstairs, and the Scottish Executive.

10 Other guides in this series

- The new Mental Health Act – A guide to advance statements
- The new Mental Health Act – A guide to compulsory treatment orders
- The new Mental Health Act – A guide to consent to treatment
- The new Mental Health Act – An easy read guide
- The new Mental Health Act – A guide to emergency and short-term powers
- The new Mental Health Act – The role of the Mental Welfare Commission
- The new Mental Health Act – A guide to named persons
- The new Mental Health Act – A guide to the roles and duties of NHS Boards and local authorities
- The new Mental Health Act – A guide for people involved in criminal proceedings
- The new Mental Health Act – Putting Principles into Practice
- The new Mental Health Act – What's it all about? A short introduction
- The new Mental Health Act – A guide to independent advocacy
- The new Mental Health Act – An introduction to the Mental Health Tribunal for Scotland
- The new Mental Health Act – Rights of carers
- The new Mental Health Act – A guide to the role of the mental health officer